W9-BZD-074

Let's Talk About Racism

Diane Shaughnessy

The Rosen Publishing Group's
PowerKids Press™
New York

Published in 1997 by The Rosen Publishing Group, Inc.
29 East 21st Street, New York, NY 10010

First Edition

Book Design: Erin McKenna

Photo Illustrations: Cover and all photo illustrations by Seth Dinnerman.

Shaughnessy, Diane.
    Let's talk about racism / Diane Shaughnessy.
        p.   cm. — (The Let's talk library)
    Includes index.
    Summary: Discusses the nature of racism, possible explanations for it, and ways to end it.
    ISBN 0-8239-5041-7
    1. Racism—Juvenile literature. [1. Racism. 2. Prejudices.] I. Title. II. Series.
    HT1521.S433 1996   96-45161
    305.8—dc21   CIP
                                                     AC

Manufactured in the United States of America

Table of Contents

The Human Race

People all over the world are alike in many ways. We are all made of skin and bones. We all feel love, happiness, pain, and sadness. We are all members of the same family—the family of the human race.

We are also different in some ways. We come in different shapes, sizes, and colors. We believe in different things, and have different ways of doing things. We're divided into groups called **races** (RAY-sez) based on our differences. But we all belong to the human race.

◀ You may meet kids from many different races at school.

5

What Is Racism?

Racism (RAY-sizm) is the mistaken belief that one race is better than another. Someone who is **racist** (RAY-sist) may treat other people unfairly or in a mean way just because they are different from him. A racist may even hate people who are different from him.

A person who is racist may say mean things to people who are different from him. ▶

Sonia and Michele

Sonia and Michele looked at the candy bars for a long time. They only had enough money for one candy bar, so they had to choose one they both liked. A man of a different race behind the counter yelled, "Hey, you two! What are you doing?" He thought Sonia and Michele were going to steal something because they looked different from him.

This is an example of racism. The man thought Sonia and Michele were going to do something wrong just because of the way they looked.

◄ Racists may think bad things based on the way someone looks rather than on the way she acts.

Why Is There Racism?

Most people are afraid of what they don't know or don't understand. Some people are afraid that people who are different from them will hurt them or take something from them. Many people don't **respect** (ree-SPEKT) those who are different from them. And they often don't take the time to learn about them. Instead, they choose to **ignore** (ig-NOR) or hate people who are different. These people are racists. There are racists in every race.

Someone who is racist may choose to ignore ▶ people who are different from her.

When Does Racism Happen?

Racism can happen at any time, in any place. You may have heard jokes at school that make fun of Asian people or white people or black people. These are racist jokes. You may have heard some kids call other kids racist names. When you call someone a racist name, you are saying that you don't respect him and that he doesn't deserve to be treated **equally** (EE-kwuh-lee). You are saying that you are better than he is. And no one person is better than any other.

◄ Everyone deserves to be treated
equally and with respect.

Where Does Racism Come From?

Nobody is born a racist. People learn racism from their families, friends, teachers, and neighbors. They may hear that certain races are better than others. Or they may hear that some races steal, and others take jobs away. They may learn that some races are dirty, or that others are dumb. These things are not true. There is no one race that is smart, or dumb, or dirty, or that steals. There is no one race that is better than any other race.

People can learn racism from their friends. But they can also learn how to get along with people of other races. ▶

Learning Tolerance

The first step in ending racism is learning **tolerance** (TOL-er-ents). Tolerance is understanding that people are different. It means respecting that difference. It means learning from people who are different from you. One way to learn tolerance is to put yourself in another person's place. How would you like to be called a name? Or be made fun of because you eat food that's different from everyone else's? Or be teased because you wear different clothes?

◀ It can be fun to learn about the holidays that other people celebrate, such as the African-American holiday Kwanzaa.

It's Good to Be Different

One of the best things about the world is that it is filled with many different kinds of people: black, white, Asian, Hispanic, and many others. Each group gives something to the other groups. We share foods, styles of clothing, and holidays. We can learn about the world by getting to know people who are different from us. It is good to be different from each other. Imagine how boring it would be if we all looked, sounded, and acted the same!

You might be surprised to learn that Native Americans gave us popcorn, and Africans gave us peanuts. ▶

Learning About Other People

Katie put down her fork and wiped her mouth. Then she said, "That was the best rice I've ever eaten!"

Anil smiled and said, "It had a spice called curry in it. My mom learned how to cook with curry in India. That's where she and my dad were born." Katie didn't know where India was. So Anil pointed it out on a map. "I hope I get to go there someday," Katie said. "I would like to learn how to cook with curry!"

◀ You can learn a lot from people who are different from you.

How Can We Stop Racism?

You can help end racism by being **aware** (uh-WARE) of it. You can also help by speaking out against it. If you hear someone telling a racist joke, tell her it's not okay to make fun of other people. Take the time to learn about the people who are different from you. You will become a better person by accepting and learning about people of other races. And you might make a new friend.

Glossary

aware (uh-WARE) To notice or realize something.

equally (EE-kwuh-lee) Of the same value.

ignore (ig-NOR) Not to pay attention to.

race (RAYS) Group of humans that is defined by their looks, customs, and traditions.

racism (RAY-sizm) The belief that one race is better than another.

racist (RAY-sist) A person who believes that his race is better than another's.

respect (ree-SPEKT) To show honor for someone.

tolerance (TOL-er-ents) Being willing to allow others to be different.

Index